# Shadowlight

# Shadowlight

Joanne McCarthy

Foreword by Madeline DeFrees

BROKEN MOON PRESS

Some of these poems appeared as they are here, or in slightly different form, in the following publications: *ArtReach, Attention Please, Centerfold, In a Nutshell, Nitty-Gritty, Slackwater Review, Washington Verse,* and *Writers Forum*. Grateful acknowledgment is made to the editors of these publications.

Printed in the United States of America.

ISBN 0-913089-05-2

A percentage of the sales of this book will be donated to Associated Health Services (Hospice of Tacoma), 750 South Market Street, Tacoma, Washington 98402.

Broken Moon Press
619 Western Avenue, Box 10
Seattle, Washington 98104 USA

*For Michael, Thomas, John, Matthew,
Kate, and Claire*

# Contents

# Acknowledgments

I particularly wish to thank Madeline DeFrees, whose generous assistance brought this manuscript to its final form. My thanks also to the publishers for their unstinting friendship and support.

—J. M.

# What Remains Haunts the Air
## Foreword

Joanne McCarthy *has the eye*. This somewhat bizarre expression alludes to one of the speakers in the mythological poem "The Gray Women." Like that speaker, the poet combines precise language, accurate intuition, and a semi-prophetic awareness that resonates dramatically in her strongest poems. Although this is McCarthy's first book, it should be clear that she has lived and written long enough to understand and communicate profound truths about the human condition. Her poems often forge some moving and beautiful order from the darker, more negative aspects of everyday life at home and abroad: a child's accidental hanging; a society more concerned with a husband's public embarrassment than with the source of his wife's uncontrollable tears; a woman, dead on the mountain for which she was named.

The style is sometimes glancing, oblique, elliptical, the lines driven as much by careful attention to sound and rhythms as to meaning, and, by that very strategy, successfully mining the subconscious.

In "The Gray Women," the poet fleshes out the meager detail of Edith Hamilton's account, giving words and voice to each of the three, who share among them a single eye and a single tooth, passed from one to the other. At the end of the poem, the story appears to merge with the Medusa myth (thus recalling Louise Bogan's famous poem)—a move that seems wildly inventive until one recalls that Medusa was one of the three Gorgons, sisters to the Graiae, and that the beholder, not the Gorgon, was turned to stone.

In "The Dreamer," written for her ill mother, McCarthy frames the poem between two pairs of lines of objective narration in a more-or-less realistic mode. After the first, she slips imperceptibly into a blend of open-casket and undersea imagery which suggests a consciousness beyond death. At the close, "the narrow room where we wait," the place of the family's vigil, becomes the sentinel post for each watcher's (and reader's) own death.

Life has its brighter moments as well, and the poet responds to them: Natural scenery, especially in her native Northwest, leads her to observe the slightest changes carefully and to articulate them persuasively in poems such as "Sweetgrass Country," "Alpine Spring," "Seascape at Evening," and "Otherworld." Most of the poems move beyond mere description to suggest the "thin / ring from another life." It is that other life as much as the present one—so fittingly celebrated in all its aspects of shadow and light—that keeps the reader coming back to these poems.

The mark of a poet's success, as one critic has noted, is that her language tends to get itself reproduced exactly. Such usage contrasts sharply with more functional and utilitarian styles. The difference explains why devoted readers of poetry sometimes memorize without even trying, a phenomenon that brings me to a further observation. Through many of these poems, the sea winds like an inexhaustible undercurrent—the analogue, if you will, for human consciousness, a blend of memory and perception that, from moment to moment, can never be captured in its entirety, but only suggested as in "woodsmoke / windchimes / echo."

Readers will, I trust, return to this book again and again until the lines become a permanent part of memory, for the poems have the advantage of being beautifully presented in a physical format that is an art in itself. Personally, I feel a debt to Joanne McCarthy and

to Broken Moon Press. The art of the poems engraves
itself on the memory; the art of the press asks us to
take the book in hand.

Madeline DeFrees
Seattle, Washington
November 29, 1988

# Shadows

# At the Inn

what you said in the dusk
about the child, seeing him
hanging there breathless, your voice
a perfect natural, the memory
familiar now, unswerving
eleven years old, a game
in the garage alone, swinging
from some cast of rope that wound
itself around his neck, all
there, the family there, and no
one missing him till no one
could ever find him

the porch swing creaked, the air
was cool and sweet, above our heads
lobelia stirred in blue profusion
I swallowed tears but you
were steady as the night behind
the mountains     only the nephew,
you said, blond hair, blue eyes,
same name, nobody thought
to ask, you ached for him
to be twelve, then it would be
over    behind the light
in your eyes, always that shadow
moved in you, a moth
at the screen, the river
over black stones

*for Mary*

# The Mourners

He has already risked everything.
He has fathered a son
    who vanished.
He has fathered another
    who never was born.
He has loved a woman
    who left him.
He has loved a woman
    who died.
What shall we say to comfort him?
He will choke on the salt of his tears.

Look: he is eating a stone.


*for Greg*

# A Grandfather

this picture frame is empty
my father's father has no face
his worn wife slipped away after fourteen children
    one born or lost each year
my nine-year-old father wept
    and begged to be buried with her

my grandfather's children did not love him
    Julia and Annie stumbled through marriage
    (anything to get off the farm)
    then Mary and Martha, Rose and Tillie
my Uncle John wandered into town
    squandered his bachelorhood in booze
    grew old in bleared surprise
my father followed the Rainbow Division
    that led into France under Black Jack Pershing
all fled that immigrant homestead
    where the old man reigned, harsh and bleak
    as a Dakota winter

my Hungarian grandfather
    squatted on his homestead
    watching his children disappear
    after his wife and the dead infants
what was on his face then, nobody knows
he was not mourned when his death came
    nor was he spoken of after
    except by my mother
    who had nothing to lose except memory

# Waiting for You

I am the sea.
You are the pearl
at the heart
of my secret.


*for Sean*

# The Dreamer

She has slipped the husk of the body,
the slick pale tubes and the needles.
She drifts in a sea-green cavern
crusted with polished shell,
the silver lilies beside her
exuding the richest odors—
musk rose, sandalwood, spice.
Fingers of sea nymphs caress her,
anemones whisper her name.
Jewel-fish red, green and gold
dart through the lace of her hair
spread like a delicate sea fan
on the iridescent water.
An angelfish nibbles her wrist,
its kiss the tiniest prickle.
Faint music, the murmur of mermaids,
echo the heart's deep chamber
in that great green cave of the sea
and she does not hear our breathing
in the narrow room where we wait.

*for my mother*

# Sparrow

drops
drops like grief from the nest
spraddles
thin legs too fragile to bear

a scrap of fluff
yellow around the bill
quivers
quivering

the others chatter
stammer from branch to branch
catch daylight
in the flutter of their throats

we feel a wind
blowing through space
the breath of centuries
our darkness

## Christus

umber on
teak and
oak on
stone hc
beckons us who wait alone
at his feet a jewel-light
bloody
ruby
stuns
the
night

# Undone

the things that women do best, she did
she cooked, she baked, she swept
billowed sheets on morning air
ironed and knitted and sewed

the things that women do best, she did
grew fertile, wept, gave birth
suckled her babies, rocked them, sang
smoothed their fears in the night

the things that women do best, she did
from dawn to dusk to dawn
scrubbing, scouring, mending, sighing
ripped from her sleep by their cries

the things that women do best, she did
but when they grew away
her face went gray
eyes flat as scattered buttons
her mouth, crazy as a crooked seam

curled in her bed
when they brought her food
she watched the empty air
and when they called her *mother mother mother*
she stitched a phantom baby to her heart

# The Gray Women

These women dwelt in a land
where all was dim and shrouded
in twilight.
    —Edith Hamilton, *Mythology*

The First:
    I have the tooth. I will speak
    though now the others cannot understand
    and I mistake their mumbles.
    This tooth sets me apart. It stops my tongue
    slipping along the sad slick gums. If there
    were apples here, I might bite into one
    and let its crisp flesh flood my mouth with
        sweetness.
    Or I might pierce my arm and suck my blood
    and curse this wretched world. This keen tooth
    grieves me, yet to pluck it from my mouth
    would twist my entrails cold.
    No one can understand this, no one.

The Second:
    This eye is mine but briefly. Now I see
    the three of us, blind, mute and trapped
    on this gray shore of rock and withered grass.
    I see my sisters hunched and miserable,
    but lacking the tooth I have no power to tell them
    what I see: that we are so alike.
    And when the eye is taken from me, I
    forget all I have seen. If only I
    possessed both tooth and eye, we could . . .
    A hand gropes toward my face. No, wait!
    I am just beginning to see!

The Third:
    I cannot see. I cannot speak. I think.
    In this sad land, everything is dark
    save when my hand clutches the eye we share
    and I can place it in my empty socket.
    When the tooth is mine I yield sometimes to
            madness,
    shriek and tear my flesh. I know two others
    wait with me, but feel no comfort, only
    the tips of their dry fingers, dusty palms,
    as we pass and pass again between us that
    which is never enough. We know
    only to protect what we cannot see
    and what, if we saw, would turn us into stone.

# Out of Place

## On the Dock at Yokohama

a brass band brays some unfamiliar tune
the Captain descends through rows of brilliant
    buttons
accepts red blossoms from kimonoed arms
and weary tourists disembark for customs
it is December and not warm
at dockside taxis wait with motors running
drivers calling loudly *Takushii!*

the old man on the dock seems out of place
a woodcut from another century
shapeless in ragged coat and patched leggings
head, feet bundled in tight strips of cloth
his muffled hands cradle a bamboo pole
with string attached, the other end
lost in murky waters of Tokyo Bay

above him looms the bulk of the great ship
behind him cranes hoist cargo, taxis bleat
still he stands mummified, patiently bent
breath pluming from beneath his scarf
waiting . . . waiting . . .

in these dark waters
Asia appears

# Exposure

on the evening train to Hachioji
a woman weeps, one hand covers her face
she clings to the pole at the end of the car
racked by sobs she cannot hold back
her grief is terrible
everyone in the car tries not to hear

beside her is the husband, dark with blood
trying to shield her from the stares of others
he does not hold her, cannot
hissing once in angry undertone
he stands so she will not fall
blazing eyes challenge anyone in the car
who dares to notice his shame, his loss of face
a wife who is publicly weeping

## Across the Bay

across the bay squat
houses, above them white wings
shatter the blue sky

## Poem for Nanda Devi,
## Dead on Her Mountain

Nanda Devi Unsoeld,
daughter of one of the first
Americans to traverse Mt.
Everest, died suddenly while
climbing with her father on
Nanda Devi (Bliss-Giving
Goddess), the mountain for
which she was named.

within her father's seed the love began
namesake of the Himalayan peak
she blooms in its shadow, dizzied by the spell
that overwhelmed her father

soon Nanda Devi begins to climb
through twenty years climbs toward heaven
yearns for the mountain
which is her self

*I cannot explain it,* she tells reporters
*there is something within me*
*about this mountain*
*since I was born*

from India, a photograph:
preparing that longed-for ascent
she stands with guide, her father, friend
her smile is shy and proud

wind knifes the mountain's northern face
slices the flesh, ices rock:
the Goddess embraces her
in terrible white beauty

then Nanda Devi reels with pain
*I am going to die,* she says
in fifteen minutes life is gone
breath cannot bring her back

pale braids wreathe her calm face
she fades beneath the snow
her heart at the heart of the mountain
where only the shadows grow

# On the Platform

at Shinjuku Station the businessmen stand
an orderly crowd of oiled dark heads
faces of ochre, bespectacled serious eyes
their blue-black raincoats spill over the platform
umbrellas, newspapers under their arms
briefcases firm in manicured hands

morning rush hour to Tokyo Station
somehow different from others
pressed shoulder to dark shoulder, each man
alone behind the private gate of his thoughts
waits for his train to arrive

# Seascape at Evening

What shore? How should I know?
　—Dostoevski

Flat trees of the Serengeti
twist away to beach grass.
Sand shifts beneath your feet.
When you climb the last dune, wind
rises to meet you, cold and steady.
Below, the great slate curve of sea
stretches forever, one distant ship
nailed to a sky too brazen,
too vast for truth.

Air grows mauve, land darkens.
Flares along the coast
beckon each other, winking out of time.
Lighthouse begins its steady pulse—
white white white, pause, a flash of red.
Turn inland to the dark.
Pick your way through shadowy dunes
to harbor where white and green stars
glide silently to shore.
Above you a delicate bat
glimmers, swoops in its fitful circle,
stitches itself to the night.

# Jishin

she dreams of rocking
   back and forth
   on mother's lap
then wide awake she hears
   harsh creaks, deep groans
   from wooden walls and floor
   a matchstick house
gently she rocks in the wide Japanese bed
   under her wedding quilt
   until the night is still
later another wave rolls over her
   but does not break her sleep

*jishin:* earthquake

# Two Views

It flattens against the wall—
blood blister, reddish-brown
size of a large man's thumb.
*Cockroach! Kill it!* I cry.
Haru-san runs to the alcove
with tiny muffled steps.
*Ah,* says Haru-san. *Ah.*
*Baby-san. Winter. Cold.*
*Mama-san die. She die.*
She pillows her head on her hands
pulls her mouth down at the corners
pretends to weep for the mother.

Haru-san stretches tiptoe
in her aproned kimono, reaches
carefully cradles the insect
carries it into the garden.
*Gone*, she says on her return
showing her empty hand.

# Keiko Returns from Surgery

The Japanese girl who has lost her womb
lies silent in a silent room.

Agony eddies around her bed
wrenching the pillow beneath her head.

Pain tautens her skin to ivory bone.
Her fingers knead a sheet of stone.

She speaks no language, she speaks them all,
turning her anguish to the wall.

In time her breath grows slow and deep,
her gaunt cheek softens. She falls asleep.

# Where We Are

## Sweetgrass Country

tumbleweeds dangle from barbed wire
in 114-degree heat or

snow piles high against the little fences
white against lead sky
for empty miles:

warm spring or early summer
when you lie on your back
in the sweet, sweet grass
watch cottonwoods hold up the sky
doze in the scent of the river
breathe honeysuckle, clover, lilac, mock orange
you come to the root of the world

# Alpine Spring

alpine spring comes late
tiger lily's spotted flame
is melting the snow

## The Lover Returns

at night he comes back
the dead lover rises
out of the grave where I've laid him
he slides by my shutters
insinuates himself under my door

he gathers himself over my pillow
and his cold flesh congeals in my bed
all night I lie wrapped in his faithless embrace
at night, only at night, he comes back

# Land's End

Water drew us
from the grassland
from the mountains
to this place.
The sun goes down in water.
All roads lead to water.

A bridge spans the water:
that tenuous steel strand
will hold for years    a century
till water
pulls it down.

Earth gives in to water.
Tide reminds us always where we are.
Everything comes to the edge
and    sooner or later
enters.

# Life Story

He said:
    I was born at seven months, beaten out of my
        mother.
    They put me in an incubator so I could survive.
    Then I was in these foster homes.
    For a long time I didn't know who I was.
    I got flashes. I would flash back
    and I could see through this glass.
    I thought it was a test tube
    and I was a test-tube baby.
    But it was the incubator.
    I would sit in the hall and cry.
    I lost two wives through divorce,
    I lost my two little daughters.
    When my third wife died, she was worth
    seven million dollars. I walked away.
    Three years ago I found my brothers.
    One is in the state hospital,
    schizophrenic like me.
    My dad beat my mother before he was born
    and he's never really been right.
    My other brother works for the CIA.
    Two extremes—and I'm in the middle.
    Mostly I think in symbols.
    I don't want to be safe.

# Otherworld

night fog
   drifts over the bridge
   rises from water
      pale ghosts
      exhaling old dreams
   shrouds steel beams in mist
   haloes mercury lamps
   muffles the cool sigh of wind

ghost-bridge suspended in cloud
   touches a shadowy shore

# The Silent Woman

When she opens her mouth, air freezes
solid like doom. Earth hesitates
on its axis, birds hang in the sky,
time rusts, wheatfields congeal.

She stands like a terrible scarecrow
with death on her shoulder, hair
straw, face pale with the sound
of no voice. The world is still

waiting for her breath to come.
Then dry stalks rustle together
and the little lives of the field
chitter.

The gold disc of moon dangles,
a sad breeze nudges her hand.
Soon snow will drift
silent
to comfort her.

# Again

after Wallace Stevens

. . . and death is the mother of memory.
Whatever we once touched, loved
stays with us when it is gone.
We hold most dear, most tightly
what we can never hold again:
warmspill of waves, mountain
lily unfolding, the baby
dead weight in our arms.

Though we may love the living
we love more what has passed us:
dark wisp in the locket, pressed
petals, moon shell, thin
ring from another life.

Memory pierces, stiletto
sliding past bone, meat and marrow
straight to the heart of things.
What remains haunts the air
like woodsmoke
windchimes
echo.

# About the Poet

A native of Montana, Joanne McCarthy now lives in Tacoma, Washington, where she teaches English and creative writing at Tacoma Community College. Her awards include a Fulbright Exchange Fellowship to Nürnberg, West Germany, a teaching fellowship in English at the University of Puget Sound, and the Writer's Omnibus Competition award for poetry. McCarthy's articles have appeared in such reference works as *American Women Writers; First Person Female, American; Encyclopedia of World Literature in the 20th Century;* and *Dictionary of Literary Biography: Modern American Poets to 1945.* Her poetry has been published in several anthologies and magazines, including *Writers Forum, Poets West,* and *Slackwater Review.*

Book design by John D. Berry.

The typeface used in this book is Imprint, designed in 1913 by Gerard Meynell, Edward Johnston, and J. H. Mason. A product of the Arts and Crafts Movement in England, it first appeared in *Imprint* magazine, a periodical designed to promote the art of printing. The type was set on a digital Linotron 202 by Wilsted & Taylor, Oakland, California. The Broken Moon pressmark on the copyright page and cover and the seal on this page were created using Adobe Illustrator, version 1.6, on an Apple Macintosh SE and typeset on a Linotronic 300. This book is printed on acid-free paper and Smyth sewn in signatures by Malloy Lithographing, Inc., Ann Arbor, Michigan. The cover painting, *Shadowlight,* was created for this book by Meredith Essex.

The publication of this book would not have been possible without the continuing generous support of Microsoft Corporation, Copper Canyon Press, and Online Press Inc.

The publishers thank the following individuals for their help in producing this book: John Berry, Tom Dean, Madeline DeFrees, David Ellison, Meredith Essex, Nick Gregoric, Nancy Jacobs, Cathy Johnson, Jack le Noir, Joanne McCarthy, Shelley Means, and Edith Walden. Book publishing is a community activity. These friends joined with Broken Moon Press to produce this work; this book represents their combined talents.